THANK YOU

*Thank you to all who have helped inspire me to write these poems.
For my husband, Larry for all his work in making this happen.
May God bless all of you with a long and bountiful life.*

Madilene Stark

Copyright © 2017 by Madilene Stark
All rights reserved. No part of this book may be used or reproduced in any manner whatsoever without written permission, except in the case of brief quotations embodied in critical articles or reviews.

Published 2017
Printed by CreateSpace United States of America
To Cover design by Madilene Stark and book layout by Larry Stark

ISBN-13: 978-1975660222
ISBN-10: 1975660226

Madilene Stark
Weyauwega, WI

1st Edition

POEMS

A CHRISTMAS SPECIAL	7
A LANTERN FOR TODD	8
CONGRATULATIONS JAY	9
FATHER & SON	10
FOR YOU MY LOVE	11
HANDS OFF	13
HEIDI	14
HEIDI'S GIFT	15
HELLO SON-IN-LAW	16
HE'S SPECIAL	17
IT'S GRASS TINA IT'S GRASS	18
JOY	19
LEATHER JACKET	20
LET HER BE	21
LET THEM BE	22
LETS GO	23
LETTER TO JAMIE	24
MESSAGE TO HEIDI	26
MIKE	27
MIKE—LET IT HAPPEN	28
MOVE IT	30
NIGHT TIME JOURNEY	31
ODE TO AN ELK	33
POEM TO GRANDMA	40
SON IN LAW–JOHN	41
"STUTTER"	42
THE BEEHIVE	43
THERE'S FEAR	44
THERE'S NO MIDDLE OF THE ROAD	45
TINA	46
TINA'S BEAU?	47
TINA'S HAIR	48
TO DAVEY	49

TO HEIDI	50
TO JAY	51
TO JOY	52
TO MY GRANDCHILDREN	53
TO MY SECOND DAUGHTER IN LAW	54
TO MY SON JAY	55
TO TERRY	57
TWO SPIRITS-TWO HEARTS	58
VIEWS OF AGE	59
WHAT IS ECHO	61
A FEW HUMOROUS POEMS	62
FAT CAT	63
I NEED TO WRITE	64
INSIDE OUT	65
ODE TO AN ALARM CLOCK	67
THE NAUGHTY FISHERMAN	68
TWEETY BIRD	69
WHO'S IN CONTROL?	70
TO MY LOVE OF NATURE	72
ANIMAL FRIENDS	73
AUTUMN PEACE	74
BREEZE	75
CAMPING	76
COUNTRY ROAD IN SPRING	78
CRYSTAL MORN	80
EARLY MORNING RITUAL	81
FALL	82
GEMS OF LIFE	83
GOD CREATES	84
GOD'S DAY	86
GOD'S GIFT	87
GOD'S PLAN	88
GRASS	89
HOARFROST	90
I'M A HUMMINGBIRD	91

LIFE	93
LITTLE SPROUT	94
MICHIGAN WINTER	95
MORNING FOG	96
MOTHER NATURE	97
MY BUNNIES	98
SKIDDLE D WINK SKIDDLE D WINK	99
SOFTNESS OF MORN	100
SUN RISE	101
THE BREEZE	102
THE HIBISCUS BLOOM	103
THE WISE CRANE	104
TODAY	105
TREES	106
WALK IN THE RAIN	107
WISCONSIN BEES	108
WISE BIRDS	109

A CHRISTMAS SPECIAL

A puppy for Christmas,
Oh what a gift
He'll come into your life,
And give you a lift.
He's chock-full of antics,
He is a playful small pup.
If you're feeling quite blue,
He'll help cheer you up.

He yips and he growls,
And tries to sound tough.
But he tires quite soon,
Looks like he has had enough
He'll crawl into your lap,
Snuggle close in your arm.
He'll settle down for a nap,
Where it's cozy and warm.

He'll give you warm love,
Like you've never known.
How nice to have a puppy,
All of your own.

MADILENE STARK

A LANTERN FOR TODD

A lantern for Todd
To give him some light.
A lantern for Todd
To shine in the night.

I gave a lantern
A long time ago,
My lad it was just like yours
It belongs to your dad.

He was a young smart boy
Like you are Todd
He was a gift to us
Sent by God.

You are like your father
You're a gift to us too
So I'm sending this little red
Lantern to you.

It will shine in the dark
It will give you some light
If you're lonely or scared
It will say "you're alright."

A lantern for Todd
To give him some light
A lantern for Todd
To shine in the night.

MADILENE STARK

CONGRATULATIONS JAY

Congratulations on a job well done.
I'm very proud to say you're my son.
Your life is yours to use your own way.
Be free and be happy what more can I say.

MADILENE STARK

FATHER & SON

You say;
Put a basketball in your hand,
And start to play.
Put a bat in your hand,
Send that baseball away.
Get down on that mat and fight.
And your son is cringing in fright.

He just wants to run,
But his father's eyes are watching.
And he wants to please you so bad.
There stands the idol of his life,
He wants to please his dad.

Now pick up that bat and swing
And the ball will sail out of the court.
But you're throwing your little son's heart away.
It's more than a damn foolish sport.

Put a basketball in your hand and dribble.
Put a bat in your hand and swing.
Get down on that mat and fight.
Now your son is learning of fear.
And responding by finding comfort in flight.

MADILENE STARK

FOR YOU MY LOVE

I walk for you in the morning gloom
The breeze gently touches my face
The red maple leaves softly open
The image of tatted lace.
The oak awaits my arrival
Standing so straight and tall
Waiting for each day's returning
They have no worries at all.

The grass is wet with morning rain
Cheerfully drinking her fill
The badger had fun last night
Creating more holes and hills.

Deer have been prancing through the fields
Feet sinking deep in the fresh plowed ground
I pass where the pheasant sits on her nest
She leans low and makes not a sound.

Paths through the woods
Are alive with song
The birds all sing in chorus
Indented deep within the trail
Is the track of a running horse.

As I look to the right
There's a stand of small trees
Their forked branches rise to the sun.
A squirrel skitters alongside the trail
From tree to tree he will run.
The pond is still as a piece of glass
No ripple I see this morn.

(CONTINUED)

The willow leans over and in the pond
A wondrous reflection is born
The delicate white violet
Peeks out of the grass
She smiles, says, "good morning
It's spring at last."

A chorus of birds fills the air
They're singing we love you
Yes, life is unfair
Each of us has a solo part
The wren sings so pretty
Straight from the heart.

The honeysuckle awakes
The blue violet appears
The cherry blossom says
"Hello world, I'm here"
The pheasant crows, the robin charms
The red winged blackbird squawks alarms.

Mother earth just smiles
As she surveys her domain
The flowers, the trees, will all remain
Forever and ever when we are gone
The woods are alive
As they join in song.

MADILENE STARK

HANDS OFF

Why worry so about your kids
You cannot form their life.
God just asked you to be standing by
When they're feeling pain or strife.

He didn't say take their pain away
He didn't say fix it, just let it stay.
It's a part of your child
Growing into an adult.
Someday you'll see
The fantastic result.

Of all of the trials
And all of the strife
They need the experience
That we call life.

MADILENE STARK

HEIDI

You came along much later
Than all the other three.
But you are a real darling
And very dear to me.

You were so independent
When you were just a little tot.
You really were quite smart
You learned an awful lot.

So your life is all before you
Use it now—be wise.
To us, my little darling
You really are a prize.

Written to Heidi Lundwall
Valentines day 1976

MADILENE STARK

HEIDI'S GIFT

I can't explain this fur to you
I don't know why it's yours
There's something very special
But I don't know what it's for.

Perhaps I'll never understand
But I know you will.
So cherish it and wait a while.

You'll know some night or morn
When you and God are still.

MADILENE STARK

HELLO SON-IN-LAW

Hello son-in-law you're really neat
Though you don't even know.
That's one of the reasons
I love you so.

You're sweet and you're kind
Nice to have around.
I think you're great
And how does that sound?

I know I say things to you
And tease you once in a while.
But I really care about you
And like to see you smile.

I think it's really neat
How God helped Joy choose you.
I couldn't have done better
If I searched the whole world through.

Your favorite mother-in-law

MADILENE STARK

HE'S SPECIAL

Now if you are a man
Where has your little boy gone?
Why have you pushed him far away
Why can't he come along?

Why can't he be a part of you
Why can't he laugh and play?
Why when he peeks his small self out
You send him far away?

Why can't you see him like he is
A special, playful soul.
Like a little butterfly
Fulfilling his neat role.

You see him as the catalyst
For all of you that's wrong.
You never hear his little voice
When he hums you a song.

Have you ever really looked at him
Have you ever looked at you?
A man, a boy all wrapped in one
Stop seeing you as two.

MADILENE STARK

IT'S GRASS TINA IT'S GRASS

GR   Is the beginning of grass
A   Is all nice and green
S   Is for so pretty to see
S   Means it's still on the scene.

T   Is for Tina who doesn't see grass
I   Is in Marquette she lives
N   Is the second letter in snow
A   Is how awful it is.

That God dumps the snow
In Tina's front yard
The back and the side yard too
I'm sure glad that God didn't make
That kind of snow for me too.

You can have that snow, Tina
I'll take the grass anyday
But hang in there honey
The sun melts it away.

MADILENE STARK

JOY

Here I am again
Your little white bunny.
Don't you think
I look like a honey?

Look how much I've grown
Just like you.
I have a partner now
And you have one too.

Can we sit in the corner
Can we keep our eyes on you?
Can we laugh and chat
About all the things you do?

Can we be a part of your life
And remember where we've been?
Can we help remind you
There's no need to be there again.

A little girl so lost and alone
Needed to find a place of her own.
So she made up a dream
Where things could be fine.
And she would be safe
Most all of the time.

That worlds all behind us
You can keep it in its place.
We'll sit right here and love you
With a smile upon our face.

MADILENE STARK

LEATHER JACKET

Cause Christmas comes but once a year
Because to me you are so dear
I tried to think of something swift
That I could give you for a gift

Tried to think of each thing I could
Then I saw you in Mike's jacket
You looked so darn good.

But my income is depleted
So here's your leather jacket
It's not quite your size
Soon you'll have a bigger one
Right before your eyes.

MADILENE STARK

LET HER BE

What do you want your little girl to be?
A ballet dancer or a celebrity?
Do you want her to be a helping nurse?
Can she be a mechanic, would that be much worse?

Or do you want her to be a sweet little girl
With a tiny dimple, and a little curl?
Do you want her to be a model so tall?
Or an athlete and dribble a ball?

Or, do you want her to be, just to be?
And to be whatever is she?

MADILENE STARK

LET THEM BE

Please let's remember that our children are people
And remember your relatives too
They are all unique special beings
And human like me and you.

Because they're our sons or our daughters
Our fathers or mothers or wife
Gives us no right or reason
To try to control their life.

We vow that we love them sincerely
And yet on their hearts we tread
They're kind and loving and lonely
And we don't hear a word they said.

Let's try to be grateful we know them
Remember our possessions they're not
God did not give them to us
He sent them to add to our lot.

MADILENE STARK

LETS GO

When folks aren't kind
They're sometimes mean

But all in all I'm glad I'm here
And glad that you are too.

So come on Gram and walk with me
We've so much life to do.

MADILENE STARK

LETTER TO JAMIE

Jamie, where are you?
Can't find you anywhere.
There is no milk on the cupboard
No clothes upon the chair.
There's no toys scattered everywhere.

No cars to step upon
I look the whole house over.
But Jamie must be gone.
I don't hear a little voice saying
"Hi! Good morning gram'.
I think I'll have a waffle
Spread with peanut butter and jam."

This milk tastes good, I'll drink it all
And have a little more.
I don't want to pick up my toys
Let's leave them on the floor.

Get dressed you say, but why gram?
I'm in my underwear.
I can't find my socks
They're scattered everywhere.

It's really not important
If your toys are on the rug.
The thing that is important
Is to feel your nice warm hug.

So come again my little friend
And stay with me a while.
I like to hear you laugh and play
And see your handsome smile.

(CONTINUED)

So Jamie isn't here today
I think he must be gone.
I'll miss him but he'll be here soon
I know it won't be long.

MADILENE STARK

MESSAGE TO HEIDI

I went for a walk this morning
And saw a wonderous sight
A seagull directly above me
Was enjoying his sunrise flight

I said," take a message to Heidi"
He said," that I'll be glad to do."
Then three more seagulls did appear
Then one more, and that one was you.

He said, "Heidi is thinking about you"
I said, "Mr. seagull, I know.
He said, "Heidi thinks you are special
She sat and she told me so."

Then a flock of geese flew overhead
As I listened to them honking
This is what they said.

"God is always beside you
He's there with you safe in his arm
He's always there beside you
To protect you and keep you from harm."

They said, "look at all the freedom we have
now you have that freedom too.
It's your very special gift
God gave it all to you."

MADILENE STARK

MIKE

Such a sad little boy
Without a special dad
He had no special grandpa
Always told that he was bad.

Always made to feel unworthy
Always made to feel a clod
Never told of his importance
Like a special gift from God.

The little boy, he did survive
And struggled through his life
Always in a turmoil
Always in a strife.

No one to say, you are okay
Until that wondrous day
When someone said, I love you
And took his pain away.

I'm a very special bunny, Mike
And I'm coming now to you
I was a special bunny
For a wise old man I knew.

So Mike, I bring you wisdom
I also bring you joy
I'm a very special bunny
For a special man and boy.

MADILENE STARK

MIKE – LET IT HAPPEN

You planted the seeds
Now let them grow.
It doesn't matter
If they're under the snow.

They may just lie
Till the time is right.
You'll not know when
Be it day or night.

Some time soon
A sprout will appear.
Be careful, Mike
Don't interfere.

The sprouts are tender
And they might break.
So leave them alone
No chances you'll take.

So look up to God
And hear him say.
"You did your job
The rest is my way."

"I know how to do what I must do.
The rest of the job is not up to you.
You've followed through the part
That was yours.
Live now Mike, you have other chores."

(CONTINUED)

"I'll take over the job that you started.
You and your family
Won't always be parted."

"Just a little time
To work on the seed.
Patience, Mike
That's all I need."

"The sun and the rain
The love that we know.
Will soon take over
And make the seeds grow."

MADILENE STARK

MOVE IT

Terry, Terry laying down.
Get up your body
And go to town.

You need to shop,
Christmas is almost here
Now hurry up,
Get off your rear.

MADILENE STARK

NIGHT TIME JOURNEY

Over the hills and round the curves
To grandmother's house we go
Jays in the lead with his Subaru
But we're going mighty slow.

Over the hills and round the curves
The Datson's going home
His motor won't run
His hoods all done
As through the back roads we roam.

Over the hills and round the curves
We don't even know the way
But we're pushing on as I sing a song
We'll make it home by day.

Over the hills and round the curves
We're on the beaten track
Jay grumbles and grumbles there
But we're not turning back.

Over the hills and around the curves
Till we hit County "A"
No more sweat, we'll get there yet
We had guidance all the way.

Over the hills and round the curves
The doe is in the back
She's deader than a doornail
And she doesn't have a rack.

(CONTINUED)

Over the hills and round the curves
Serenity Acres I spy
We had a good trip, without a slip
And Jay is quite a guy.

MADILENE STARK

ODE TO AN ELK

My son called and said," Mother dear,
I'm going on an elk hunt this year
Would you like to tag along as my guide
Or just come along for the ride?"
I needed a little time to ponder
I packed my bags and we headed down yonder.

Down to Atlanta, across the bridge
The terrain was nice, first a hill then a ridge.

The D.N.R. in that place ain't slow.
They said, "to orientation you must go.
You can't shoot our elk if you don't know how.

"Sit down and we'll give you some pointers
No multiple kills, no beast left to rot
You clean and take home the elk that you shot.
If you have a bull tag you can look for a rack
If you shoot the wrong elk, you'll never come back.
If you're hunting a cow, you better make sure
That whatever you shoot is not a him, but a her."
"We'll help you," the D.N.R. said.
"Don't disobey the rules or you'll wish that you were dead.

"We might take your truck, your gun or money
Your trip back home won't be joyful or funny.
You are helping us here to control the herd
Do follow the rules, we have the last word."

(CONTINUED)

DAY ONE;
So opening day we're all fired up
We packed up a lunch and jumped in our truck.
As we ride along out to section E
We're baffled and lost, we're from the U. P.
Pretty soon we find our way
Should we believe what the D.N.R. say?
I don't think their elk count has been right
There is not a cow or a bull in sight.

Along about noon I whisper, "look there,
It might be a stump, but it wiggled an ear."
Then Jay says," Oh, Ma, you're so eager to see
A big old cow, that you're fooling me."
He looks and he peers the way that I beckon.
Then he drives on ahead and says," Ma,
I reckon we'll stop and eat lunch then start hunting again."
Then I say, "stop this truck, there is an elk in that glen."
He finally sees what I have been spotting
Just then the elk gets up and starts trotting.

As he stops and looks back
We both start to laugh
he's so pretty and graceful
But he's just a young calf.

So on through the day we hunt
And We wonder
we know there's a calf, now
Where is his mother.

(CONTINUED)

Then Jay looks back and he yells
"Oh no, our trailer is sitting back there in the road."
From all the bouncing these roads have given
Our trailer a trouncing.

We pull off the road, it's time for repairs.
We are not hunting now but who the hell cares.
The weather is crispy, it's breezy and cold
I decide now is the time I need to get bold.
I decide it's time to be wild and free.

I drop my hunting suit and take a good pee.
As I lean over with my mind in a muddle
The sleeve of my suit soaks up the pee puddle.

An hour and a half spent in repair
Tomorrow that trailer ain't going nowhere
The first day of our hunt
We've seen eight bulls and a little calf runt.

DAY TWO;
A fresh new morning we're back on the hunt
We want a big cow, not a little calf runt.
The trailer stayed home, back at the shack
So we're tearing along, the four wheeler in back.

The C.O. says we can't use it no how.
But we'll use the damn winch to hoist up a cow.
With Jay's bad back and mine pretty weak,
A hip that aches and an ankle that squeaks,
A shoulder with spurs and not the best eyes,
Maybe this elk hunting trip was not wise.

(CONTINUED)

But what the hell, we're down here now
And we aint goin' home without gettin' a cow.
Today we're believing somehow
If there's so many bulls there must be a cow.

If that's not true in rutting season
There'll be no reason for you buglin' and wheezin'
We park our truck, a runway we see.
Jay says, "oh, boy, that's where I'll be."
That's not the way they hunt elk here
But we're really programmed from hunting deer.

A red truck drives by as we sit here and wait.
The D.N.R. says, "Don't shoot before eight."
A few minutes later I hear a blast
I'm hoping that Jay saw a cow at last
Driving past us that guy was quite wise
He saw 20 cows just over the rise
We wasted no time following their trail
But we never saw a head or a tail
We then took a road where we couldn't survive
If we didn't have a four-wheel-drive.

The road narrowed down and we came to a halt
The next thing that happened was nobody's fault
We tried to turn, it was quite a squeeze.
Jay says, "I can't see to turn, ma', are there any trees?"
Now it seems to me that I once told that child
In a forest like this the trees grow wild.

(CONTINUED)

They don't run and get out of the way.
They stand there firm, day after day.
When one of them connected with our truck door
That truck door wasn't smooth anymore
We decided it was time to call it a day
We got out of that road and went on our way.

When we opened the door as we got back to camp
Everything felt cold and damp.
The furnace was out, the sink froze up tight
It wasn't a good day, it's not a good night.

DAY THREE;
We drive out early to the clearcuts
Through the muddy road and the slippery ruts
We spot some elk, they're quite far away
We hope to find a cow today.

As we look through our glasses we don't have much luck
Wherever we look we just see a truck
Today our excitement is not ebbing and flowing
Our hope of bagging a cow is going.

DAY FOUR;
Another day to hunt for a cow
We want one today but we don't know how
We decide to not move from the section we're in
We really don't want to start over again.

(CONTINUED)

We're a little late getting started today.
But we climb in our truck and get underway
We are discussing today where we will hunt
We don't want a bull or a little calf runt.

At the next gas well we see elk, oh great
We look at our watch, it's nine minutes to eight
So we drive on by, park down the lane
Then sit there and wait, nine minutes of pain
The longest nine minutes that ever have been
Anticipation is bounding, we're excited again.

The snow softly falling the day is great
We head for the gas well hoping we're not too late
The elk are still there, Jay climbs out of the truck.
They look like cows I think we're in luck.

Now Jay says, "Ma', take the truck and drive on
We'll fool these elk into thinking were gone."
So I drove up the road as far as I could
And I turned around as I knew I should.
I saw Jay standing on the road with his gun
So I thought that the job was all done.

I expected to see a cow laying flat
But the rest of the story doesn't go like that.
The cows were moving down the ridge
And Jay was standing right there in the ditch.
As I drove up and stopped in the road
I didn't know Jay's gun still had a full load.

(CONTINUED)

He started waving his arms, his face got red
I can't repeat the things he said
Right then I knew I better move on
Before any signs of those cows was gone
I drove on ahead stopped for a spell
Did he shoot one yet, how can I tell?

Then I heard a blast and right then I knew
Before too long that big cow elk would be stew
She didn't go down as quick as she should
She escaped us and ran a half-mile in the wood.

But being the kind of hunters we are,
We tracked, praying she'd not go too far
Finally her head showed through the trees
And Jay's next shot brought her to her knees.

She was down and the hunt was all done
We knew she wouldn't get up and run
As we look at her lying there
My throat felt a lump, my eye felt a tear
We both were in awe, couldn't say a word
But we knew we were helping control the herd.

MADILENE STARK

POEM TO GRANDMA

Grandma, grandma, she acts so silly
She is 60, but acts like a filly
She combs people's hair with a toilet scrubber
Farts in public and blames her hubber.

We love to have her here with us
When she leaves we throw a fuss.

HEIDI LUND WALL—ABOUT MOM

SON IN LAW–JOHN

He flew to an area remote
To discover the depths of his heart
He already knew that the things he must do
From his love he had to depart.

So each could look at a heart, his own
And discover why each remains alone
Now each had to look for the key to his heart
For things that are trying to tear them apart.

Life's lessons are so hard to learn
We stumble and fall don't know where to turn
But then in a twinkling it all comes quite clear
Just be who you are live in love not in fear.

MADILENE STARK

"STUTTER"

Stutter Jason stutter
Stutter till you want to shout
Stutter Jason stutter
Till you feel you're inside out
Stutter Jason stutter
Laugh into it's face
Stutter Jason stutter
With a smile upon your face
Stutter Jason stutter
You can beat this in the end
Stutter Jason stutter
And it will become your friend.

There's a reason for your stutter
You're a chosen one, my boy
So Stutter Jason stutter
One day you will see the joy.

Each time you stop and stutter
You're learning something new
It's God now preparing you
Big things in life you'll do.

So Stutter Jason stutter
Hold it close now to your heart
Stutter Jason stutter
It's your super special part.

MADILENE STARK

THE BEEHIVE

DEAR HEIDI & KURT

This beehive represents your love
It's so delicate and rare
Put too much pressure on it
And it can be crushed
Maybe beyond repair.

As you see
It's very unique
In design and color
That's because it's the only one
Exactly like this
The same as your love
It's only yours

You can share part of it
But some of it is just for you
I see you both as this beehive
So delicate, so rare
God's gift! I love you

MOM

MADILENE STARK

THERE'S FEAR

There is fear like a knot
In a mother's heart
The fear also reflects
In her eyes
She hears there is war
In the middle east.

She says what will this mean
To my son he is my baby
I brought him into this world
I trained him to be kind and true
Now he's headed into the war
Now what does a mother do?

MADILENE STARK

THERE'S NO MIDDLE OF THE ROAD

There's no middle of the road son
There's no middle of the road
You can't carry around each half
It's just too much of a load.

You have to choose this way or that way
You cannot live here and there
There's no middle of the road, son
Now that you know how you care.

God said "set aside your possessions"
And set them aside we all must
You know you can't go on divided
There now is a God you can trust.

There's no middle of the road son
If you're there you'll know what I mean
So accept now the plan that you've wanted
There's really no life in between.

MADILENE STARK

TINA

She brought all the stuff out
And left it on the table
Her mother screamed, "Tina
Clean this up while you are able

If it's still here
In the early morn
You'll wish to hell
You were never born."

MADILENE STARK

TINA'S BEAU?

Now Tina met a handsome lad
Her eyes were all aglow
His hair was long his jeans were torn
His earring hung down to his arm
When he opened his mouth
He croaked like a frog
Tina said, "oh God
This guys a dog!"

MADILENE STARK

TINA'S HAIR

Tina tried to crimp her hair
She couldn't get it right
She said, "I can't go to school
I look like such a fright!"

Her mom said, "I'd like to help you
But I'm at a loss of what to do
Do you see that wall socket there
Just stick in your finger
And you'll have crimped hair."

MADILENE STARK

TO DAVEY

DAVEY,
Some people don't like morning
Some people don't like night
But you will like the morning
If you get up feeling right
So hang me up by your bed
I'll be there every day
When you see me in the morning
All your frowns will go away.

Madilene Stark

TO HEIDI

The Sun's coming up
I'm thinking of you
I'm feeling you're in so much pain
But I'll leave you alone
Let you work it through.

Our friendship will remain
You've been gone a long time
Or it seems like it's been
But I have a feeling
You'll soon be home again.

MADILENE STARK

TO JAY

Thank you, Jay for being my son
What a wonderful man to lean upon
Whenever I'm in distress or blue
I know that I can call on you.

All I ever want you to do
Is to raise your son to be like you
When his mother needs a helping hand
Her son will be there to understand.

MADILENE STARK

TO JOY

We were hoping for a little girl
When you came into our lives
You were a precious little child
And now you are a wife.

You'll soon become a mother
And your life will be complete
You'll have a child like we had you
And it will be so sweet.

So go on now and live your life
Be happy every day
Keep your smile always near
Don't let it go away.

MADILENE STARK

TO MY GRANDCHILDREN

To my grandchildren I've had many stories to tell
These stories our history but not to sell
A gift to be held or shared with their own
When they're eager to listen or partly grown
I have spunk when I need it
And I know when to give
I'll continue to be me
As long as I live.

MADILENE STARK

TO MY SECOND DAUGHTER IN LAW

Although you're the second to join us
You're still just as dear to my heart
I hope that you and our son
Will never have reason to part.

If I had searched the world over
If I had looked through and through
I know I couldn't have found
A daughter-in-law like you.

So remember to come if you need me
If you ever have trouble, my dear
I'll help you in all ways that I can
And promise to not interfere.

MADILENE STARK

TO MY SON JAY

What's the matter with you
Son, you're okay
What's the matter with you
What do you say?

Why are things so negative
Why must things go wrong?
Why can't new things be happy
Why don't they bring a song?

There's a so so chance
That things will be okay
Why must you expect
They'll go the other way?

Why when you hear a new idea
Your first reactions—no
Why can't that be changed to yes
And then let it go.

For all the years you've been this way
Why don't you make a change?
Only you can sort this out
And maybe you can rearrange.

Your life will be so easy
You'll not need to fight
Things won't be the same
Neither black or white.

(CONTINUED)

You will see the middle ground
And if you stop and look around
At all the good things about your being
I think then you'll start seeing.

If we listen carefully and if we dare to look
We'll see most things are positive
I read this in a book.

The book was given to me
By a man–I call my son
The day he gave me that book
New life for me had just begun.

So in this package you will find
A book that's just for you.
Read it son, from front to back
And be surprised at all it will do.

Mom

MADILENE STARK

TO TERRY

Although you are son number two
You are very close to my heart
You should know that in my life
You are a very important part.

You were always fun to have around
I enjoyed you every minute
So thank you for being my number two son
My life has been great with you in it.

MADILENE STARK

TWO SPIRITS-TWO HEARTS

Joy came to visit me
She's okay, so pretty to see
Inside she has a very loving heart
We're never very far apart.

Miles really don't matter
When hearts are in tune
It matters not how far
The sun from the moon.

Stay right in line
They seem to be in sync
That's the way it is for Joy and I
At least that's what I think.

I know when she is feeling bad
She knows when I am blue
The miles don't really matter
Our hearts just stick like glue

Our spirits travel hand-in-hand
They flit, each gets a lift
Two hearts that often beat as one
A mother daughter gift

MADILENE STARK

VIEWS OF AGE

At 6 she's oh so sassy
12 Is a persnickety age
At 15 she's considered rebellious
Terrible two is just a stage.

At 72 she's senile
At 50 she's over the hill.
At 6 months she's crying and screaming
She's a child with a very strong will.

Life begins at 40
39 is Jack Benny's number.
At 90 she's close to dying
Allowed to nap and slumber.

At 17 a delinquent brat
God, how did numbers get labeled like that?
At twenty she's ready to marry
She's college material too
At 30 she should stop having children
What is she trying to do?

18 Is the door to freedom
By 60 you're just too old
At 4 she's sassy and cute
At 5 she's getting too bold.

At 90 she's tired and wearing out
At 75 she's a dear
What goes with a certain age
Has not been made very clear.

(CONTINUED)

At 13 a lady, at 10 a brat
How can we switch things around
Like that?

25 Is thought of as settled
At 40 let me be free
I have to search and find out
What is really me.

These numbers are driving me crazy
They're just labels in my head
I wonder what label I'll receive
When at 100 I turn up dead.

MADILENE STARK

WHAT IS ECHO

Echo is an echo of me
A little spirit
That needs to be free
Confinement can't be
A part of her life
If captured she'll suffer
Grieve, sickness and strife.

A spirit to flit
From here to there
It always must be
Going somewhere
So much to learn
So much to see
My granddaughter Echo
Is an echo of me.

MADILENE STARK

A FEW HUMOROUS POEMS

FAT CAT

Fat cat, where are your babies?
We're patiently waiting to see
How many babies you're going to have
Will it be five or four or three?

Jamie is patiently waiting
You can have them while he is around
I know, fat cat, the projects yours
We're kind of impatient I've found.

Jamie will be here till noon
That's all.
So fat cat, please
Get on the ball.

MADILENE STARK

I NEED TO WRITE

The house is burning down,
But I need to write
I can't help it
If it is the middle of the night
When I write, I write, and I write.

I hear a siren
The smoke's getting thick
To write in this mess
Is quite a trick.

My husband just jumped
Out of the upstairs window
The fire hose slid across my desk
I wish they would quit all this yelling
And give a writer a rest.

How can I write in such a squall?
A fire ax just came through the wall
I picked the damnedest time to inspire
Ouch, I've got to go, my rear is on fire.

MADILENE STARK

INSIDE OUT

Did you ever stop to wonder
How the flip side really looks?
Of all the things you see in life
If you saw them in reverse?

To be inside an apple
Would the seeds look very big
If you were inside an oak tree
Could you see the branch or twig?

A fish from the inside must be
Guts and flesh and bone
Did you ever see the backside of a scale?
In either a small fish or a whale.

If you got inside a motor
Would you hear the gush of oil
Would the sound be overwhelming
Could you hear that engine toil?

Now what about a pillow
With feathers soft and warm
Would you giggle while they tickle
Either on your leg or arm?

How about a can of peaches
Would you slip and slide around
Would you drown in all the sticky juice
Could you even hear a sound?

(CONTINUED)

And then inside a head
With brains scrambled all about
Would you think of railroad stations
As the trains go in and out?

And how about the onion
Would the odor be too strong
Would your eyes begin to water
If you stayed in there too long?

Now birds are oh so delicate
They are wonderful to see
How would you feel inside a bird
While he sits up in a tree?

Inside a rose inside an egg or even in a heart
Inside a whale, inside a snail or even filling up a tart
Inside an ant, inside a plant or inside a little boy
Inside a sassy female that's always acting coy.

If you were in a pickle jar
Would you be a dill
If you were in a wallet
Would you be a dollar bill?

Now did you ever stop to think
How different it would be
If we could change things all about
And I was you and you were me?

MADILENE STARK

ODE TO AN ALARM CLOCK

If that thing had a neck
I would squeeze so tight
I'd teach it to be quiet
In the middle of the night.

I'd really like to sleep
I'm in a dream, there's no respect
Or so it would seem
What it is that causes
That darn thing to scream?

I didn't touch the button
That turns the blamed thing on
I wasn't looking forward to
That early morning gong.

I bet it was my husband
That put that thing in gear.
Tonight I'll say, "now honey"
And he'll say "what is it dear?"

I'll turn to him with drooping eyes
And say "you great big lug,
When I turn in this evening
I'm going to pull the plug."

MADILENE STARK

THE NAUGHTY FISHERMAN

A secret lure
He held in his hand.
But I think he lied
No fish in the pan.

He'll boast and brag
And cast here and there
No sound of a captured fish we hear
And he flailed out plug after plug
I could have caught more
On an old dry bug.

The mighty fisherman at his best
For supper there's chips
Couldn't catch the rest.

Into the minnow bucket he reached
Popped open his eyes
Said, look at this minnow
He's a pretty nice size
He dropped in his lure
I heard a small thunk
His secret lure was the tail of a skunk.

MADILENE STARK

TWEETY BIRD

I found a little tweety bird
Living all alone
I said, "little bird I know a nice lady
Who will give you a home."

He acted really cautious
At first would not agree
The little bird was lonely
So soon he trusted me.

The lady liked her little bird
She tended to his every need
She gave him lots of water
And kept him in fresh seed.

Alas, he was so happy
He flew down to the floor
A troop of healthy joggers
Came running through the door.

Tweety wasn't very alert
His thoughts were all on you
The last thing that he saw
Was the sole of a tennis shoe.

MADILENE STARK

WHO'S IN CONTROL?

Did you ever see a puppet
Hanging from a string
Controlled by someone's hand?
The puppet might say
I think I'll walk
But the string says
No, you will dance again.

The puppet might decide
To wave goodbye
But the string says
You must nod hello
The puppet might want
To kick up his heels
But the string says
You must go slow
The puppet thinks
I feel like crying
The string puts
A smile on his face.

The puppet is tired
Of hanging and keeping
This terrible pace
The puppet just wants
To be at ease
And smell the flowers
And see the trees
And smile and see
The clouds in the sky

(CONTINUED)

The puppet can't just
Enjoy the land
Because all the control
Is in the hand.

MADILENE STARK

TO MY LOVE OF NATURE

ANIMAL FRIENDS

Now I have animals all over the place
They're a great asset to the human race
The dogs outside, the cat's in here
To me each one, is very dear.

I talk to the horses when I go out
They never holler or never shout
They're really happy to see me too
They don't care what I do.

The ducks in the coop come out to say
We're very glad you're here today
They look at me and think of feed
I always tend their daily need.

They quack and romp and have some fun
Sometimes I wish that I was one
Animals have no cares or strife
They just are happy to live their life.

MADILENE STARK

AUTUMN PEACE

Do angels paint the leaves at night?
When morning breaks the trees are bright
They stand there bright in every hue
As they glisten in the morning dew.

And among the colors there
The greens are nestled everywhere
Nature's picture is oh, so real
The presence of my God I feel.

Decorated forest by many paints
The work was done by heaven's saints
The beauty there, in all it's splendor
Is just God's love, so sweet and tender.

MADILENE STARK

BREEZE

Softly, softly wafts the breeze
Majestic in its power
Gently touching leaves on trees
It knows no time or hour.

Playfully flitting here and there
Joyful in its splendor
Shifting here and shifting there
It knows no space or gender.

Freely touching free to flow
Softly on its way
Dancing, slipping to and fro
Welcoming each day.

MADILENE STARK

CAMPING

A camping trip's a delightful thing
For the kids and a man and his wife
But when the bugs fight for your blood
It can be a terrible strife.

It's nice to get up at the break of day
To see the beautiful sun
But as soon as the tent zipper makes a sound
The bugs are there on the run.

The no-see-ums are the tiniest ones
So of course they are the first to be fed
A nip here and a nip there
From our toes right up to our head.

Then the mosquito steps in and says it's my turn
And the little ones all disappear
Now with mosquito when he moves in
At least a warning you hear.

As the day wears on they all take turns
There are new kinds every year
The no-see-ums, the sand fly, the deer fly
Oh dear, oh dear, oh dear.

The fishfly, the horsefly, the green fly
Are there, all awaiting their turn
By now we are all scratching
And our hides are really starting to burn.

(CONTINUED)

The Ranger says, oh no we can't spray
There is just too much confusion
Then in our parks they better start
To serve instant blood transfusions.

MADILENE STARK

COUNTRY ROAD IN SPRING

As you walk with me on my country road
Look at the wonders of spring
A Creek swollen with melting snow
A bobber free at last

Water flowing so unencumbered
A bird silently dipping his beak
A red winged blackbird
Performing his passion of spring.

Fence sagging, long forgotten
Tangled by grapevines
Heralding spring sweater itching
Rabbit footprints and spring night.

I see green sprigs bravely
Extending their heads
Like children sneaking a peek at Santa
Cow bawling awaiting birth.

Tame geese crying wanting to join wild honkers
Cattails standing in majestic clusters
Begging spring to give them new life
Chill wind saying–not yet–not yet.

Dogs barking in distance for freedom
Yellow house–quiet.
Chickens salvaging remnants of last feeding
I smell the rotting cornfields waiting for the plow.

Proud weeds – remembering summer
Robin flitting from tree to tree
And ground bragging about spring.

(CONTINUED)

Winter wheat awakening peeking through snow
Puddles–ditches–all in readiness
Ducks skipping across pond alerted to flight.

MADILENE STARK

CRYSTAL MORN

Crystal blades of grass as stiff as the dead
Weeds that look like angel wings
Raise their dainty heads.

The fields are iridescent, a chill is in the air
Mother Nature's been at work
The signs are everywhere.

The beauty of this early morn
No artist's brush could do
World of glistening stillness
Thick with morning dew.

I stay so still and quiet
I must not break the spell
Softly as I tiptoe by
I feel that all is well.

MADILENE STARK

EARLY MORNING RITUAL

I hear the whir of the dragonfly's wings
As he watches his shadow in the pond
The breeze blows him gently off course
His life span is not very long
He hovers in the air as he meets his mate
A pretty damsel fly

He can chase ripples in the pond
Or soar high in the sky
A tender mosquito is a breakfast feast
A morning cruise on a floating leaf
New morning new day no cares no strife
Live to the fullest, that's the meaning of life

MADILENE STARK

FALL

Flocks of birds playing in the sky
Fall is here–time goes by.

All around I feel the breeze
Colors settling on the trees.

Fall is here–time goes by
Birds are saying, time is nigh
Come, let's fly.

MADILENE STARK

GEMS OF LIFE

A little bit of heaven
Put here just for me
I can choose to share it
Or just to let it be.

The trees sway softly in the breeze
The wind whispers sweetly through the trees
The path is strewn with surprises
Where will it finally lead.

MADILENE STARK

GOD CREATES

When God did create
The hearts of the field
No shackles he placed
No ties he did wield

Choice of freedom I give you
Take it embrace it
And do what you'll do

So the creatures accepted
This gift at a glance
Then loved it, enjoyed it
Saw no need for advance.

We are the ones who change things about
We either want to get in or want to get out
No, never content to be where we're placed
But we my friends, are the human race.

Cats don't fight wars
Bombs aren't made by dogs
Chickens don't pretend
Abuse not done by frogs.

Foxes don't lie
Sheep don't boast
Doesn't bother them
If they end up in a roast.

(CONTINUED)

They live what they are
They be what they'll be
Looks like very good teachers
For you and for me.

MADILENE STARK

GOD'S DAY

There's nothing like sitting
Beneath a tree on a summer day
Feeling the tender touch
Of the breeze.

The birds love it
They're so cheerful today
They sing and skip and praise God
Thanking their creator
For all the splendor.

Oh how little we humans know
We were made to be like the birds
What have we done to our blessed peace?
I need to stay here
Need to write
Need to remember.

MADILENE STARK

GOD'S GIFT

Just a little bit of beauty
In this little Jasper stone
Share the beauty with some others
Or enjoy it all alone.

It's a little bit of heaven
Cast upon a sandy shore
So enjoy this pretty little gem
God has left us many more.

MADILENE STARK

GOD'S PLAN

Why did God put animal creatures on earth?
Maybe to help us to see our worth
I think as a child how I was loved by a dog
At that time of my life, even love from a frog.

They're full of love, they don't hold back
They will kiss you, or lick you, or jump in your lap
No need to pretend when there is nothing amiss
Just living life in a state of pure bliss.

From time to time I've questioned their reason
To behave like they do in a given season
Now that I take a more definite view
I don't think it's behavior, I think it's just do.

They do as they are, they do as they please
Be it scratching the door or feeling the breeze
We are the ones who put in the stops
Then put ourselves down and call ourselves flops.

Did you ever see a failing dog
Or a divorced cat, or an abusing frog?
Did you ever see a dog with a bone
Concerned and afraid to eat it alone?

No, I really don't think that these things are true
why should they partake in the things that we do?

MADILENE STARK

GRASS

I plucked a blade of grass today
And looked at it in awe
As I gazed upon that blade of grass
This is what I saw.

Each section meant another day
Or another year, could be
And as I gazed upon that grass
I thought of you and me.

Now life is like a blade of grass
Each chapter something new
Exciting things and happenings
Surprising things we do.

Sometimes there's pain
Sometimes there's strife
Sometimes there's so much more
Sometimes there's things that we don't like
Sometimes we close the door.

But like the blade of grass
We can stand majestic in the field
And just accept each happening
Whatever life may wield.

MADILENE STARK

HOARFROST

Crystal blades of grass
As stiff as the dead
Weeds that look like angel wings
Raise their dainty heads.

The fields are iridescent
A chill is in the air
Mother Nature's been at work
The signs are everywhere.

The beauty of the early morn
No artist's brush could do
World of glistening stillness
Thick with morning dew.

I stay so still and quiet
I must not break the spell
Softly as I tiptoe by
I feel that all is well.

MADILENE STARK

I'M A HUMMINGBIRD

I'm a hummingbird with spirit so free
I will hover quite near
But please don't capture me
I get just so close
Be glad that I'm near
If you reach out to grasp me
My heart fills with fear.

I stop for your sweetness
Leave you some of mine
From flower to flower
In the race against time
But never no never
Try to stop me in flight
If I'm captured and held
My life can't be right.

I was made a free spirit
To fly and to soar
Now fly here beside me
I won't ask for more
You're my friend
And I love you
But I'll be what I'll be
You've helped me to become
What really is me.

Little hummingbird
Little hummingbird
Your cage is all gone
You're lifted up high
You're sailing along

(CONTINUED)

Nobody confined you
Your cage was your own
You built it around you
To remain all alone.

MADILENE STARK

LIFE

Life is like a river
Flowing gently by
The ebb and flow continues
Till the day we die.

At times so calm and peaceful
At times the waters rough
At times life is so serene
At times it's plenty tough.

As we watch the river
It just flows gently by
No need to really get upset
No need to wonder why.

The rough spots or the smooth ones
Are all a part of life
So live them as you meet them
There's no time left for strife.

MADILENE STARK

LITTLE SPROUT

Little sprout continue to grow
You came so far yet so far to go
God made life a continual thing
We can choose to cry or choose to sing.

Pain is here pain is there
But it's cushioned with joy
And with people who care
Imagine the pain when something near dead
Opens it's eyes and lifts up it's head.

It can look at life all around
And hear the world a delightful sound
Now see why I'll see you as a sprout
The beautiful Kerry is coming out.

MADILENE STARK

MICHIGAN WINTER

It's twenty below zero
And all through the house
Every board is creaking
I'm as cold as a louse.

The car won't start
And the water won't run
I really don't think
That this weather's much fun.

I sit here and dream
Of a warm sunny beach
While the temperature falls
Right out of my reach.

But then in the sun
You might get burned
If you stay out too long
And I never learn.

So I'm better off here
As I shiver and shake
I might turn blue
But at least I won't bake.

MADILENE STARK

MORNING FOG

We walked in the field this morning
We walked in the field in the fog
We walked in the field this morning
Me and my Labrador dog.

The sky was soft and heavy
The fog gently touched my face
The dew hanging on the grass
Looked like angel lace.

The field was so inspiring
There was so much there to see
We walked in the field this morning
My Labrador dog and me.

MADILENE STARK

MOTHER NATURE

Did you ever have an oak leaf caress your arm?
It's like the touch of a mother loving and encouraging.

Mother Nature croons blue bells ringing
In sync with the breeze
Snort of the deer as he sounds alarm
All is not as it should be.

Something invades the area
Listen closely I can hear the sound of my hair
Blowing in the wind.

Endless chirp of the wren
Catbird crying in the distance
Everywhere I go I hear wrens
Sound of my father calling
Protecting me.

Letting me know he is near
White Eagle calls as he did many times long ago
I heed because of his great love
Father, Father, Father, God.

MADILENE STARK

MY BUNNIES

I need to share my bunnies
I need to let you see
How very soft and precious
These bunnies are to me

I need to let you touch them
To feel them soft like silk
You need to watch the mother
Feeding little ones their milk.

Their eyes are oh so pretty
So soft so bright and pure
Beneath their chins hangs
A soft round ball of fur.

They're such tender animals
But still protect their own
They can live as a family
Or be happy all alone.

They seem so adaptable
To each new situation
They're such a charming
Example of God's creation.

MADILENE STARK

SKIDDLE D WINK SKIDDLE D WINK

Oh, how I sometimes hate
To think about all
The things that fill my head.

Like unpaid bills
Floors to clean
Meals to cook
And clothes that need washing.

Beds to be made
Sweeping to do
A husband to kiss
And even more.

Wax to put on the floor
To make it shine
And on and on
With household tasks.

But damn I want
To walk outside.

Commune with Mother Nature
Hear the birds
And see the deer
To feel the breeze upon my face.

MADILENE STARK

SOFTNESS OF MORN

Softness of morn sprinkled with dew
Birds awake, life starts anew
The trials of life seep in all day long
By midday it seems, the softness is gone.

The evening breeze blows gently by
The trials of day begone
The moon shines bright and I await
The softness of the dawn.

MADILENE STARK

SUN RISE

When I see the sun rise
I always see a barn
It seems like every sunrise
Should come up over a farm.

The suns coming up
I'm thinking of you
I'm feeling you're in so much pain
But I'll leave you alone
And let you work it through.
And our friendship will be again.

You've been gone a long time
Or so it seems like it's been
But I'm feeling you are now quite near
So do what you need
And when you are done
I'll welcome you home special dear.

MADILENE STARK

THE BREEZE

Softly softly wafts the breeze
Majestic in it's power
Gently touching leaves on trees
It knows no time or hour.

Playfully flitting here and there
Joyful in it's splendor
Shifting here and shifting there
It knows no space or gender.

Freely touching free to flow
Freely on it's way
Dancing slipping to and fro
Welcoming each day.

MADILENE STARK

THE HIBISCUS BLOOM

When I open the door
In early morning light
I am blessed by God
With a beautiful sight.

The hibiscus blossom
Stares at me
Oh what a glorious thing to see

I planted her by my back door.

MADILENE STARK

THE WISE CRANE

As I sit and watch the cranes
They are doing what cranes do
They are not copying birds
Or complaining of the dew.

They are doing crane things
In the world they are their own
They need not stop to question
They never stop to moan.

They live in now and live in here
They wonder not they show no fear
They're doing crane things
That is clear.

MADILENE STARK

TODAY

Crows are crying
Birds all trilling
Woodpecker tapping away
Hum of civilization is faint
Nature is first.

Blades of grass waving to each other
Alfalfa showing its head
Looking forward to fall harvest
Too soon, too soon
Spring has just arrived.

MADILENE STARK

TREES

Did you ever talk to a tree
Or feel them alive like you or me
Did you ever hear them scream in pain
When a power saw rips into a vein.

Have you ever watched them slowly die
Or bow their head and seem to cry
As a bulldozer pushes their roots aside.

MADILENE STARK

WALK IN THE RAIN

We walked in the rain this morning
The field was all fresh and green
As the clover tasted each raindrop
They knew when the rain was ore'
The sky would make a drastic change
And the sun would come out once more.

We walked in the rain this morning
My dog, Rufus and I
Each tender raindrop touched my face
As it gently fell from the sky.

Now are raindrops angel tears?
Angels don't have reason to cry
But the raindrops touch so lightly
As they fall so soft and shy.

Now maybe raindrops
Are just a touch of love
Sent down to us from heaven
From angels and God's love.

MADILENE STARK

WISCONSIN BEES

Wisconsin has a lot of bees
There on the flowers
In the trees.

When summer comes
And we sit outside
They're in our hair
And on our hide.

Beware if they get
In your can of Coke
If they stay in your throat
You might even croak.

These little covers
Are made by my hands
To keep those suckers
Out of your cans.

MADILENE STARK

WISE BIRDS

There's nothing like sitting
Beneath the tree on a summer morn
Feeling the tender touch of the breeze

The birds love it.
They're so cheerful today
They sing and skip and praise God
Thanking their Creator for all the splendor

Oh, how little we humans know
We were made to be like the birds
What have we done to that blessed peace?

I need to stay here
Need to write
Need to remember.

MADILENE STARK

Look for
OVER A LIFETIME
A Book of Poetry: Volume 2
by Madilene Stark

Made in the USA
San Bernardino, CA
18 January 2018